WICKER BASKET MIND

POEMS BY
D.L. WHITE

EDITED BY
CANDICE LOUISA DAQUIN

ISBN: 978-1-9168779-4-8

Artwork by SueAnn Summers Griessler

Book design by Scissortail Press scissortailpress.com

*This collection is dedicated to my wonderful
friend and fellow writer Saniyah Khan
– Bunny –
stolen from this world so young*

I miss you everyday.

Forward

I became acquainted with Danny's work when I edited his first novel. Subsequently I have worked on his second novel and during this time, voraciously consumed his poetry. I quickly came to see why he is so well respected in the writing world. Wicker Basket Mind is his second collection of poetry, comprised of some of his hard-hitting pieces that set the social media world alight. It is the element of poetry most neglected, and most needed: Searing testimony of recovery from a male perspective.

Sometimes the only respite to a cruel world is to transform pain into creativity. The capacity to harness horror and transform it creatively to share with others, is exactly why books like this must exist. How many men have no outlet, no comparison, no way to stop feeling isolated? How many end up taking their own lives because nobody told them, you are not going through this alone? What have we as society done to help men who suffer in silence? Carrying the atrocities like daggers in their hearts, hurting themselves and others because of how badly they were hurt? Dying before their time because abuse goes on long after the physical abuse has stopped.

If one person reading this book comes to realize they are not alone, and it saves them from giving up and taking their life, then the purpose behind these writings has been achieved a thousand-fold. I suspect the legacy of this collection goes even beyond saving lives.

Books like Wicker Basket Mind demand that we do not turn to apathy. The only way things change is if we reveal them and stop pretending it doesn't happen. When you read Danny's work you see he's made that commitment to his art, and it shows in the consistent quality and creativity he's able to produce. I'm continually impressed by his devotion to his craft but there is something even more impressive than that. His willingness to share and elucidate the horrors he, and others, have been witness to.

Ask yourself what it takes to expose those deepest wounds on your psyche? And then ask yourself how we as a society have let this carry on through millennia? Being a father himself, Danny has thrown the gauntlet down and cried out for change. His poems are testament to his determination to be that change for his own family.

Danny's writing is challenging, visceral, unfiltered; it demands our attention. Despite the serious nature of the subject, do not assume this collection is pure darkness and suffering, because ultimately, I came away feeling a strong sense of redemption, hope and possibility. That is the ultimate gift, to remind us, whilst they may have nearly died in the fire, like a phoenix they flew out of the flames and defied those odds. A survivor gives us hope, and brings learning and wisdom. It is their legacy now; one of healing, and commitment to over-turning pain and cruelty. In this book we find a man we deeply admire, deeply respect and wholly believe in. This is his voice in the uncompromising medium of poetry. Hear him.

Candice Louisa Daquin, Writer, Editor & Psychotherapist

Contents

"I have to write because
if I don't get something
down then after a while
I feel it's going to bang
the side of my head off."

— Terry Pratchett

Acknowledgments

Of the many people worthy
of acknowledgment I shall
name but a few…

The Literary Pages Assembly

Emily for editorial and
ethereal guidance

Candice for seeing me

Mira Hadlow who extracted
me from darkness

Stuti for buzzing around me
at all times

Robert for your foundation
of wisdom

SueAnn Summers Griessler
for the artwork and
friendship

Poetry can be measured in two ways:
how real it felt,
or how real it made you feel.

– D.L. White

Introduction

Thank you for choosing my words and supporting my writing journey. The thought of another human holding my words in their hands (or on the screen) fills me with gratitude. Wicker Basket Mind is my second solo poetry collection.

The main theme (or perhaps non-theme) to this collection is my endless love for words and the power they can wield. You will find it all in these pages: joy and pain; darkness and light; love and loss; highs and lows; melancholy and hope; quiet reflection and noisy revolution.

With this collection, I didn't feel a need to sectionalise the poetry as I wanted to show you – the reader – that my mind is like a wicker basket, weaving itself around itself in often random, always wonderful, ways.

As a note to the reader, some of these poems have been written in character(s) from different perspectives, other than my own. Some of the poems are dark, raising challenging subject matter in uncompromising ways. As such, this collection should be read with a cautionary trigger warning for tragic content.

I truly hope you enjoy reading these pages as much as I enjoyed writing them.

Again, **thank you** so much for choosing my words, and supporting my journey.

First Words

Innocence is lost:
you can find it under fingernails
of beasts who poached it
from me.

I spent my childhood in pain,
my teens wondering if it was my fault,
my twenties fell aside to drugs and denial,
hoping intoxication could flush agony out of me.
My thirties, I played therapeutic catch up
talking myself into deeper nightmares,
trying to reason the pain away.
It never did.
It never will.

Memories were locked in metal cages;
rusted recollections,
slipping from consciousness.
Words fidgeted on incarcerated tongue
behind a prison cell made of teeth.

For so long
fear twisted
itself around my spine,
crippling and constricting me,
addling me with agony
anytime I tried to move forwards.
I learned to exist in stasis —
without angering the beasts wrapped around me.
I reserved expression

for trauma temper tantrums
and self-harm fits.
Pretty little wrists
and sunless forearms
tattooed by self-loathing scars.

I screamed a lot:
Into cracked mirrors,
pillow cases,
wine glasses,
and toilet bowls.

I fucked a lot:
boys with barking mouths
but bite-less souls,
bragging their way into bed
apologising their way out the door.

I cried a lot:
under searing showers
coiled up like a snake,
ready and begging
to shed sinful skin.

I bled a lot:
pebbles of plasma
pooling in puddles
of ravenous red.
The first time I wrote a feeling down
was with maroon paste;

I let my quivering finger-quill linger
in the bloody sludge ink.
I wrote on a broken mirror,
"Please kill me"
It was a short poem;
polite but to the point.
It only got one like.

After that,
creation's floodgates
burst open –
tsunamis of traumatic water
crashing against rocky conscience,
sculpting jagged stones
into countless little stories,
little verses,
little words,
of my life.

Cages melted –
words released
from my thought prison.
My mind became a prism
of repressed expression.
Rainbows of pages
formed by luminous ideation
catching on howling rains.

Some words charged
like a rodeo bull

on a furious rampage.
I tried to hang on,
keep in control,
but the bucks and kicks,
spins and twists,
we're too much too quick.
It made me physically sick,
Then better after.

Some, words are like firework displays
exploding kaleidoscopes
of blazing lights
against dark skies,
leaving smoke and silence
in their aftermath.

Trauma was shaken loose
from atop my memory mountain
In aching avalanches –
decades of rotten remembrance
surging down slopes
into piles of compost,

nourishing my truths
with words and verses.

Some of it sits in the sediment
of subconscious depths,
waiting for aching extraction.

My mind is simultaneously
a dream factory
and
a graveyard,
where ghosts of dead memories
haunt the promise of fresh starts.

I can't yet explain this properly –
I can't explain myself properly.
I can't explain anything,
only write,
until it's all written out.

Which I hope is never.

Lamb

I am a lamb in wolf clothing;
behind this monstrous veneer
scared sinews fidget in fear.
Beneath scar tissue and gristle
beats a barely audible heart.
I'm not afraid like a kitten;
I'm afraid like a lion six days into starvation,
feeling the weight of doom
in weakened flesh and bones.
Heavy like lead, from leading.

Half the time I'm bored –
pretending to want things,
wanting to love things.
Half the time I'm bleeding –
fighting to forget things,
yearning for an ending.

I express emotions;
syllables on to pages
in dark blood language,
thoughts forged in fire,
but what about the little girl –
the one making chains
out of daisies?

I never cry
for help,
or for attention.
I cry out of sight

of prying eyes,
to myself
and to her —
the one who
hadn't fallen yet,
hadn't wanted death yet.

Where can I find her thoughts
in this **wicker basket mind** of mine?
What am I afraid of?
That she was braver than me?
That she was a warrior,
fearless and free?

I wear teeth on my sleeves.
I howl at silver circles in the sky,
to protect her
from them;
to not let them in.
But she doesn't need protecting —
for, she is still a wolf,
and I am but a lamb.

[Inspired by Mira Hadlow]

Treading Water

Not all wounds heal.
Not all loads lighten.
Some things we learn to carry.
Some pain we must bear –
burdened but survived.
Folded but still alive.
The passing of time
is a test of strength,
and sometimes,
treading water
is the best
we can give.

Private Darkness

We're all drifting,
aware but aimless,
heavy with intent,
too busy for action.
Poking cheap fun
   wherever
we don't feel it,
   wherever
hurt burdens others.
We try our best
surviving this public circus,
melting in private darkness,
tip-toeing
over eggs shells,
ignoring elephants in rooms,
igniting our own fires,
warming our faces
so, we might face this
incessant madness —
arching our backs
under the weight
of being things
they want (us to be),
buying things

we don't need,
searching for worthiness
where worth is just a number.
Filling lonely gaps
with social solitude.
Filling chat rooms with people
we have in common.
Emptying our minds
for fear of losing commonality –
being the same as everyone
is confused with being normal.
Sameness stifles progress,
whilst difference folds over conformity.
Firework minds
made to feel dangerous
    and deviant.
Static minds
rewarded with greatness
    and fame.
Made to feel clueless,
starving for information
from angry news channels,
with pre-packed thoughts
modulating our minds.

Our endless hunger is for truth –
the fear is not freezing to death,
It's not trying to start the fires.
Bartering dying breaths
for our desperate chests;
taking hope from the choking smoke.
Breathe it all in –
blow it all out.
Are you losing
or winning?
Sinking
or swimming?
Do you live in denial
or deny you are living?
Light isn't just within –
we're supposed to be
each other's light.
Sometimes you are the day,
holding a torch to another's night.

Never Enough

It can never be enough:
there will always be more
I should have given you.
More I could have done,
or tried to say.

How can it be possible to requite such love?
How can any token compare to how you make me
feel?
The beat you give my heart.
The calming of my stormy mind.
The agony you borrow from my bones.
The way you always take the load.
The finger tips and kisses in happy hours.
The touches and clinches in dark times.
The way you were yesterday;
the way you'll be tomorrow.

Requital is futile;
I must accept I am destined
to never quite measure up,
and always let us down.
In the end,
Some things fall apart;
The stitching of wounds
stops the bleeding,
but the scars,
   the scars,
      keep breeding.

Too Much To Ask?

Is it too much,
to want to feel love
the way the tides
feel the moon –
to possess love
the way the moon
possesses tides?

Holding the very balance
of you
    in my gravitas;
the very rhythm of your life
    in my loyal orbit.

Knowing my sudden absence
    would cause you such devastation.

That I'd take with me:
the very warmth from your flesh;
the beat from your heart;
the oxygen from your breath;
the will from your bones;
and you'd fold,
into equal halves
sorrow and desperation.

That I'd leave starvation on your skin;
an itch only my nails can scratch –
the hanker of my touch
meeting you with insanity.

You, become a ravenous babe,
craving the milk of my affection.

Is it too much –
to expect barren parts of you
be quenched by my tidal emotions;
to dream your locked away desires
are keyed open by only my lips.
To imagine that your feet cannot dance
without the melody of my body beside you;
that you cannot make love
    without my amorous hands
        to guide you?

That you'd stare blankly
at empty spaces,
sobbing at silences
    I left behind.

That you'd willfully wilt away –
for, you would rather slowly fade
than exist outside our love.

Like a wind-up toy
    you'd sit listless,
        waiting for me
            to turn the key.

Is that too much to ask,
    instead of lying there with her?

The only way to free
a bird from a cage is
to destroy the cage.

Paper Bird

Have I ever mentioned the girl
with quirky bones –
tongue like liquid gold, licking ignorance
into ingots,
splitting the difference
until there's nothing left to split?
The one pressing ink
on papyrus wings –a paper bird
breaking its back
on smeared glass ceilings,
folding over, trippy footed
versions of herself
to become like everyone else,
but she never can.
An extraordinary girl
can never have ordinary days,
can never sew or bake cakes,
and sit unsatiated
on apron strings.

Feeling damned
and dumbfounded;
stale and numb.
Just—Done.
Feening for release
from finger tipped incarceration.
A glove –inside out –
soft lining
facing the world.

Porous mind glistens
(In reminiscence)
like high noon reflections
on spring break lakes;
dipping skinny
wearing nothing but water and moonlight –
speaking nothing
but witchcraft and war.

Dumbing herself down
to meet tepid minds.
Mollifying decadence,
dulcifying her shine;
Covering big thoughts
with small smiles.
Peeling back personality.
Too big.
Too snarky.
Too hysterical.
Too smart.
Too MUCH.
Taking off shoes
to stand shorter –lesser –
Sacrificing herself
at asinine alters:
fake a smile, fake a dumb mind,
pretend to not care about the things
broiling inside.
Purse your lips
around wasteful words –

Don't speak of truth.
Don't speak of change.
Stay calm., stay the same.
Play the game; play badly enough
to remain unnoticed,
well enough to drown.
Well enough to hate.
Well enough to negotiate
a middle rung
on lethargic ladders,
leading to despair
but not destitution.
Place passion on a shelf
for now; just for now —
still for now. Still. Stay still.
Save that face
until the wind changes —
until it's wise enough
to stay cold; old enough
to decompress.
Until it's too late.
Too late.

Once fountainous youth
trickles into follicles,
silvering the roots,
calcifying intention into frigid rock —
washed only by vicarious seas.
Shift your eyes
from anything you desire —

anything worth having.
Focus / ambition / drive.
Don't look up (too far);
it's only sky anyway,
and why look at sapphire skies
when you can mind
your business?

Porcelain face, out of place –
mustard on the wrong sandwich.
The songs you like, don't play anymore
at parties too young, too modern,
too high octane for you.
You're not like them –
but the teen with quirky bones
and golden tongue
still dreams, still dreams she is
like them. Like everyone
except herself.

Sitting stiff in places
where they don't notice you,
surrounded by people
without the necessary eyes
to understand such majesty;
such Amazonic poise, as yours.

All the things that hurt you,
the things that formed you,
framed you, forged you,

melted and moulded you –
caged you.
That forced you
here and now to
be an ongoing origin story.

Paper bird;
holding paperbacks in back pockets.
What's the point of a paperback
If you can't show it to the world?
Show them you're a reader.
You're a believer
in magic and mystery,
love and disaster.
In something: Anything…
    …but the truth;
anything…
    …but the ache;
Anything…
    …but write.

[Dedicated to Candice]

Taking the Flowers

If I must drown –
if that's my inevitable fate –
I'm taking the flowers with me;
something pretty to look at
whilst my lungs swell with water.
I think it will be the lake;
not the bath.
The bath holds too many memories –
to many reasons to care.
To many reasons not to.

If, by magick,
I emerge from submerged
a new and brutal
version of me,
full of knowledge and savagery,
ritualistic black blood
seeping with my steps:
be scared, child –
tremble in fright.

For, I will return as death
dressed in night.
The howls
(and bowels)
of a thousand Alphas
fueling my fury.
The seas will simmer
in anticipation
of my awakening.
Trees will bend a path for my return.
Soils will scorch under sacred footsteps.
The sky will hold thunder for me;
unleashing crimson rain
at my blinking command.
Do not stay and fight:
  run;
    run;
      run;
cut and run.

[Dedicated to MJ]

Crownless

This is for the princess
without a crowning queen;
a mother whose own mother
cursed the family streams.
For the girl who made daisy chains
In secret, and unseen.
Who made grown up claims
and never got believed.
For the one who dares to fly
despite the tattered wings.
To the woman setting fire
to generational disease.
For the crying babe
cribbed in thorns,
whose love was noosed
in blooded applesauce.
To the lamb in wolf clothing
eking out a witchy craft,
working in her shadows
dreaming light upon her back.
To the unpainted toes
of the girl who ran,

from broken bones —
from the 'family' man.

To the girl too young
to raise a child.
To EVERY choice.
To EVERY chance.
To EVERY loss.
To EVERY mile.
To the one who held
a still beating heart
that slowly folded
into the dark.
To the ones
without a prayer,
to the ones
without a womb.
To the rubbery chair
in a sterile room.
To the grief.
To the scars.
To the wishing upon

bleeding stars.
To the cut.
To the run.
To the daughter.
To the mom.
To the moon.
To the son.
To the only just begun.
To the one;
To them all.
To the rise,
to the fall –
To the writing on the wall.
To piñatas
that become
soaring unicorns.
To the lighthouse on the land;
to the ship lost at sea.
To the crownless.
To the crowned.
Know I love thee.

Language of the Lost

There is a secret language,
ancient and Un-divine,
very few can claim to know.
It's not in words or phrases,
practiced prose or versatile verses.
It's in hieroglyphic wounds
that etch out pain
on thinning skin.
It's in eyes;
once warrior eyes
that danced and thrived
and sought retribution –
now black and lost-lonely,
as though the universe
placed sterile voids
where soul-windows used to be.
It's the throated sounds
of moving mouths
without passion or purpose.
Baseless tones
of 'hi' and 'hello';
high and low,

low,
    low.
In the subtle corners
of pink flesh
where numb muscles
cannot express;
cannot be coaxed to form
an appropriate smile
(A frown clown).
It's the absence of a joke
where one used to be;
reeling back your words
from your tongue tip
because offence fears
become deaf ears.
Silence can't offend;
silence can't be bent
around whispers,
in rumours,
in voices you hear
or don't hear.
Quietness becomes salvation;

until you can't find quite enough quiet.
Even cemetery silence
feels obnoxiously violent.
Noise,
   noise,
      noise.
Even graveyards have songbirds;
warbling their love,
lamenting their loss —
curiously oblivious
that their tweeting
bounces between
tooth shaped headstones
of dead sons and daughters.
They do not understand
their juxtaposition,
any more than those
without secret cyphers
can comprehend
the language of the lost.

Scorched Lips

I hoped
kissing demons would scorch
your name from these lips,
but tasted retreating syllables
of your name on my teeth.

I hoped
demonic tongues would lick
purging flames,
blistering you from my skin,
but I felt your name
in goose-bumped braille
with lost fingertips.

I hoped
the touch of fiery hands
would char
your essence from my flesh
but the smoke
stank of you.

I hoped
allowing them to possess me
would replace,
or expel, you,
but every quiver
of muscle memory
held on to your name.

They became versions of you;

their breath became your breath,
their touch became your fingers,
their scent smelled like your perfume,
their groans your grunts,
their screams your lies,
their faceless skin-suits
became you.

The syllables of their names
melted and reformed as yours.

My moans of pleasure
fell into tears
of losing you.

I hoped
that drinking whiskey neat
would wash
your noun away
but your letters clung to my throat
like limpets of loss.

I hoped
that the drugs would erase,
or sedate,
the memory of you;
you became grey clouds
looming heavy
waiting to rain down
in sobriety.

I hoped
the parting
of skin on wrists
would release you,
from my bloodstream
but I sat in a puddle of our pain,
weak and alone.

I hoped
the fall would exorcise you
from my tormented soul,
but the last sounds
from my burnt lips
were screaming
and pleading
your name.

I hoped
that death
would be enough,
but I was forsaken
to haunt you.

Black Sugar

I try to take little fairy steps,
but my chest churns demonic breaths.
My mouth is a furnace
of melted cotton candy desires.
My mind is ablaze
with chaotic raging fires.
The flames lick at my synaptic nerves.
The sweat beads on feline curves.
I want to release myself:
unload this black sugar passion.
Give you sweet stained satisfaction.
Moisten your membrane with molasses.

I feel them flutter;
the wings that used to define me.
I used to want to fly above it all;
the stink and mess of happenstance.
Now I let it rattle my bones
and wet my skin.
I exist inside and thrive on it.
I am that saccharine succubus;
sweet on the tastebuds
bitter in the aftertouch.
I won't demand much,
just your total devotion;
apply it like syrup lotion.
Hold me down and drip it on me –
give me black sugar baby.

Skin Deep

Because...
I'm human I do,
of course,
yearn to be beautiful.
Not in the ways
of small minds
or swollen loins.
I yearn it in the way
a new tree
stretches its roots
before its leaves,
coaxing life from
soil;
so that on days
when the sun doesn't shine
vibrance still flows.

But beauty makes me prey;
my fruit drips
primal seduction
just as first sin
fell upon Eve
in Eden.
I don't want you to see me,
like stars;
I want to be seen
the way the moon is seen.
For folk laws and curiosities
to be borne from my existence.
I want you to howl at me

and pray that I reply.

Beauty isn't dream dust
or stories in books.
I cannot survive
on your fantasies alone.
I need to be worshipped
at altars of memory;
each prayer a currency
by which I may trade
reverence for survival.
For beauty is nothing
if not survival;
survival of the fittest.

I don't want to be controlled;
my beauty hanging
as a slow noose
around wrinkling necks.
Being dressed up
every fucking day
like lonely dolls;
as pretty as someone else's
indoctrinated vision of me.
Desirable the way
convention dictates I be.

I want to be fucking beautiful
without feeling ashamed for wanting that.
To be desired in carnal ways

but not hunted like soft prey
for easy meat.
There should be a chase
where I'm not running
from badly raised demons
and half-dressed ghosts.
My body shouldn't
explain itself to you
or require an excuse
for its existence.
My choices shouldn't set
pious tongues lashing.
My clothes shouldn't
raise concerns in courts.
My curves shouldn't
come with ratings
or warning labels.
I am not a lady in waiting
for a husband
or to be raped
because I'm beautiful
enough to deserve either.

My right to be beautiful
always seems to belong
to someone else;
everyone else
but myself.
They allow me to rent it off them
for the right price –
a submissive slut
or ladylike.
I never own it;
I borrow bits
and wear them like glitter,
for angels to wince
and demons to devour.

Sex Appeal

I wish I was interesting
In the good way:
in the way that turns heads
and coaxes hands between thighs.
I want to fill their minds with yearning
instead of just disturbing
images.

I'm fascinating,
like a lab rat scurrying in a maze;
movements observed and noted
with detached clinical devotion.
Devoid of connection or emotion.

I'm seductive like a scab,
singing itchy serenade music
to your spine.
Touch,
but not too much,
or you'll make it bleed again.

I'm addictive,
like pressing your tongue
against a mouth ulcer –
see how far you can push the pain
until it's unbearable,
until it stops feeling good.

I'm exhilarating,
like standing at the edge
wondering what would happen
if I just jumped.

I'm irresistible,
like the wet mouth you get
just before your guts clench
and, retch up your breakfast.

I'm enticing,
like a sharp blade –
the thoughts of ending it all,
without being noticed
or missed.

Happy ending?

Darling, right now I'd settle
for a mediocre beginning.

Three Minutes

Can you feel me
in any given moment,
like frigid rain showers
pelting at your skin?
I can feel you
like a beast in my belly,
simmering towards boil.
Love, it came to shake us;
I'd hoped it would make,
not break us,
but here we are
worlds apart,
no new horizons
or fresh starts.

All that's left
are the stolen breaths
we never truly owned.
Two hearts, once one home,
now, my blood flows homeless.
The hopeless pump in our chests
beating separate rhythms –
desperately discordant
disconnected recordings
of separated severed souls.

Tears of crimson silk
wet sorry cheeks:
droplets of loss
dripping from wrists.

A bone pen dipped
in thick sanguine ink
to write rancid love notes,
or hopeful death notes,
only to your ghost.
I'm in love with your ghost;
the thought and feel
of your memory
shudders seismic ecstasy
through the molecules of me.
Your love gives me motion sickness;
rotten emotion sickness.

I took medicines
to sedate you from my mind,
blind folded my senses
but you remained:
an apparition in my cognition;
a porous poltergeist;
a pulverising, plasmatic, phantasm
of lost languid limbs.
Unremembered shapes
edging off a costal shelf
of tasteless hate.

I awakened in April,
blue peeping through
cotton wool skies,
wondering how and why
I lived that bitter lie,

believed your loving lines,
wearing lyrics like band aids,
betrayal like a bandana,
false hope like fools gold –
all glitter and no shine.
I yours, you not mine.

I learned to read between the lies:
between the beats of black hearts.
To dances in the silence,
between notes of love and death.
Death greets me like a melody.
Life depletes me like a tragedy.
You treated me so badly.
I worshiped you so sadly.

Only time will tell
the story of our breaking;
The inglorious separation.
Whispering moon petals
contort to tortured howls;
werewolf and wild,
timid and mild.
One given moment,
two stolen breaths,
three minutes shy
of forever.

Fools Gold

He had a mouth full of brass promises,
lies on the tip of silver tongue –
he placed their dreams in glass boxes,
filled their heads with fools gold.

He tethered truth to false emotions.
Printed love on arrested hearts.
He tied knots around intentions,
whispered thoughts of fresh starts.

He'd been built on bravado
and raised to never care –
an insatiable, hungry ego,
caddish swagger and flare.

He talked of road trips and white beaches,
fast bikes and sensual guitars.
He stood just outside their reaches,
but stalked infatuated hearts.

He stole the music from their bones
and played it back as connection.
Wore their devotion like French cologne
and picked their pockets of affection.

He laced his words with want and trust
and softly licked their scarred souls.
Sowed seeds of coerce and suggest
sprouted saplings quivering in cold.

He showered them with anaemic fluids,
pinned their stems to jagged walls –
plucked and pruned precious pieces,
clutched petals in his mucky paws.

He dealt them front row validation –
affirmations of applesauce applause.
They confused desire for adoration
and sought his fire for warmth.

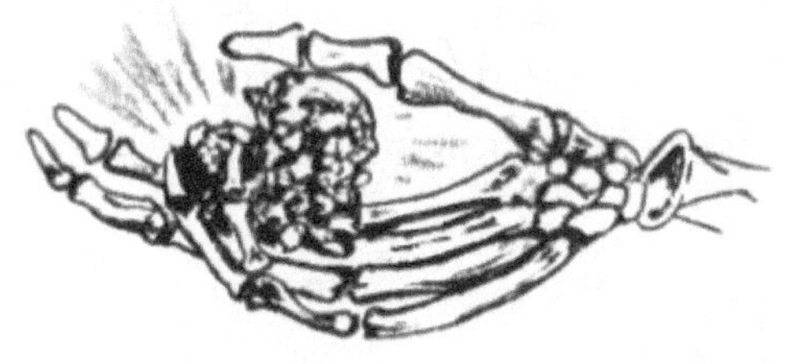

Still Selfish

If tomorrow your sky is no longer blue
know, please, that I yearned for you,
to feel only happiness of every hue;
know, please, that I loved you.

How often do you hear a person say:
"It was all my fault. I'm sorry"?

Maybe neither of us was   the one
but you were   someone
to me. And I blew it.

I don't have excuses
but I do have reasons, and regrets.
None of it was your fault:
it's not your fault I'm rotten;
it's not your fault I'm broken;
they broke me, not you.
They filled me full of bewilderment;
served me love on the edges of nails.
Wrapped cords around my throat;
choked hope from my breath.
It wasn't your fault that tender sex
held hands with brutality in my muddled mind.
That closeness triggers trauma
and lust triggers shame.
That I can't tell the difference
between good goosebumps and miserable ones.
That running is automatic, and fighting is survival.
That I could coil up like a snake and strike without

warning.
That trust was a currency
I never knew before you,
and my debts liquidated us.
I didn't understand that people could
actually like me, without it being a trap.
You didn't raise your hands
even when I held bladed threats
to your Adam's apple.

You carried
the weight of my baggage
until it crushed your chest.
I saw your eyes as you left:
once endless portals to heaven
now black and despondent;
arrested by failure.

it's funny,
all the broken bones, cuts, bruises
and split gums, that others gave me,
don't add up close to the wound
Of losing you.
The hardest pain to bear
is the empty space in my world
Where you should be.
Thoughts of you tide softly
in my oceanic mind.
I keep you in a memory box.
I open it to remind myself

how beautiful you were –
how soft yet strong. How I was wrong.
   And you never needed to be right.

If I had 24 hours with you again
I would spend it remembering
every inch of your skin.
I'd hand you books to read,
just to hear your voice,
calm and in love, not the airless tones
you said goodbye in.
I'd make waffles how you like them –
   that's a lie –how I liked them.
Because you always compromised
for me
and I didn't bend an inch
for you.

And here I am, still selfish,
listing the things that I want to do;
because I'm still learning
what love is,
what peace is,
what I am.
I hope you are happy;
you deserve a life
I couldn't give you.

I'm sorry —
I'm sorry today.
I'm sorry yesterday.
I'm sorry tomorrow.
I'm sorry.

November Rain

Winter screams start my day.
The sun makes valiant efforts,
hurling itself against shortening night, toward
daybreak,
but darkness still owns the world, as its shadowland.
I'm beginning to shiver; the cold is calling to my
bones.
Concrete clouds swell with howling rain
threatening downpours of petrichor heaven.
Thunder barks like hounds of sickness
seeking to cull and cut me apart.
October apparitions glisten in brain condensation,
dripping Ideations on rusted recollections:
hand prints of hallow-eve shenanigans
ghost across the window panes.
Cellular debris of yesterday's glee -
but it's November rain now falling,
emulsifying the last leaves of Autumn,
confetti desires melting to mulch.

Featherless thoughts
get caught in flightless cages —
the walls are way too thin
for the weight of missing him.
The way he fitted me so, so perfectly
colours me in sadness. I'm in debt to despair.
The beauteousness of Autumn
folds in to a poisoned paradise.
My cold cortex flounders in a vortex
of venom. Monochrome melancholia —

The great grey void. A bottomless pity-pit
where my sadomasochist soul
dines on its own demise.

But still I float, in endless optimism
of fresh starts and new beginnings.
Smoke & mirrors, and us,
lost in faulted pathways;
the sum of in-between. I deserve to dream.
WE deserve to dream: of the future,
of each other, or of another lover
fucking you to sleep.
Amputated love making, absent of connection.
Fingertip delusions, masking rejection
with lusty affections.
She's graceful in lace, hateful when waiting.
A stunt-double lover who wakes
to empty chiffon sheets,
and traumatic pancakes.

My breath mists the window,
and aching velvet fingertips
gracefully trace shapes on steamed glass –
hearts and kisses
that only I, and November rain, will ever see.
I press my lips to the freezing pane
and imagine your harsh winter arriving
to kiss me back.
Winding November embers
retain a vague memory of warmth.

I retreat and replete –
(S)mother myself in simple things:
books, sugar and natural flames,
lose myself in pillowed thoughts,
let the head-mess unravel, like a ball of yarn.

Returning stronger, as I always do,
In this my penultimate form.
For, I am the night –
the one who hung the moon; strung her up
by a callused heartstring noose,
the umbilical cord attachment
quivering to my cruel earth.
I am the demon on your shoulder,
you, the angel on mine,
destined to repeat these mistakes
until death.
I am sorry, my love,
in the way a bumblebee has sorrow
for the petals dislodged
whilst seeking sweet nectar.
In the way a tree regrets
the shadows of its canopy.

I'm so lonely —
desperately alone.
I'm not sure
I'll ever escape this black hole,
but I know I'll try,
I know I have to try:
for her,
for him,
for us,
for them,
I promise
to keep trying.

No Future

How does it taste –
    my name, in your mouth?
Does it set salivation
cascading against teeth,
like expensive steak
at our favourite restaurant?
  Or, is it burnt bitter,
like over-done toast
the morning after laying in the wrong bed?

How do you wash it down –
with wine your papa couldn't afford
or cheap cider,
on park swings
Tasting like a cold winters kiss of death?

I feel our past fade to no future.
Our favourite songs
once sparked discos in excited muscles,
now whimpered in harmonic bones –
dampened in our marrow.

Death makes angels of us all,
even if fallen from grace,
but we can't all be angels;
if we were,
who would write about the angels?

Without you I'm in half;
my sentences sit incomplete.
I know which words you would have said,
    just as I know every inch of you
        by heart and fingertip,
            but will never touch you (again).

She Plays for Me

When the sink-holes of life
suck essence from my soul
   – energy feels like a burdening blanket.
The woes wind around each other
into a helix cord of calamity,
wrapping around my breath,
snapping pleas for help
from my throat,
before they can fly free.
     In those moments,
          she plays for me.

When bloody ashes of the past
reignite in torturous trauma tantrums;
the edge of blades flirt with my veins
     with one flick;
mouthed muzzles promise an end to troubles
     with one click;
pill bottles rattle rhythms of release to
my inner peaceless pieces.
     With one swig;
to drown the devils ideation away,
          for me she plays.

When tears salted mother's milk,
her lavender breast like wetted silk.
when the husk of youth
fell away from my fruit;
his guitar played tunes for me
    with one chord;
his hands translated love
    with one touch;
trust trembled under dark lust
    with one thrust.
With petals falling
    from shattered abdomen
        she played for me.

She plays for me;
    don't give up.
She plays for me;
    don't give up.
She prays for me;
    rise up.

Equinox

They named the days,
when light and dark are
equally long,
Equinox.
Meaning: equal night.
That's when we tell the quiet Moon
she is just as pretty,
(and important)
as the blazing Sun.
The vernal version;
a moment of breathless teetering
when the swelling weight of spring
surpasses the strength of winter,
and the sins of frozen months
give up their murderous clutch
to a purging delight –
sponsored by love and light –
manifesting as hope;
the new life
of spring begins.

I can't help thinking
Winter performs
the hardest graft.
The honest toil;

covering and cleansing
over indulgences
of other seasons.
Death and decay,
scorched earth,
mausoleum mud.
Liquidating the canvas clean
so that the frolicking
of Spring
may paint Summer's
capricious needs
upon the still warming graves
of Autumn.

Fresh start
means
start again,
and again,
until spring is naught
but a false promise;
equinox
is the day we lie
closest to naked truth,
but dress it up
as magic.

Life After Death

I don't know what happens after death
    – no one really does –
but I do know it can't be any better,
or worse,
than this life.
No heavenly promise
can hold a light
to the cherubic hysteria
of a baby's laughter;
cackling with innocent joy,
not comprehending why.
No angel
    – of any god(s) –
can hope to achieve such purity.
No corners of hell
can hold darkness tighter
than the walls constructed
around my pain.
No deadly invention
offers worse intention
than the crevices
of my twisted mind.

What if I were to reincarnate?
I suspect I'd be neither delighted,
nor disturbed,
by the outcome destined to me.
Perhaps I'd be a great whale,
peacefully flowing through oceans,
yet constantly threatened by cruel men
with horror harpoons
and barbed moral compasses.
Maybe a lowly mayfly,
packing life into just one day;
at least free of the burden
of tomorrow or yesterday.

It's all a matter of perspective;
death looms heavy to those living 'free' –
whilst those looking over broken shoulders
often find forwards a hopeless direction.

Once Upon a Never

Once upon a December moon
all my dreams did not come true.

Do you really think little girls
only dream of being lost princesses –
yearning for a prince to slay beasts?
Is it too hard to imagine some girls are warriors?
That snarls and catcalls do not
fill us with fear,
or fright,
or lust,
or bend our pretty bones
under the weight of thoughts
   of
      big bad wolves
        and scary monsters.

Do you really believe
without your warmth
our bodies will
succumb to cold?
We'll just freeze and fold
without your testy-fires?
Should we therefore wait
for your humble offerings
of coats,
and one night stands,
to guard us from creeping winter?

Do you think an unmarried hand

can't possibly function on its own?
As if diamond rings are secret codes
to placate all fears and woes
of those
with wombs.
And do you suppose the womb maketh the woman?
That purpose hangs from an umbilical rope of
servitude,
for quivering
feminine hosts.
Or, wilder still,
there may be those
whose spirit doesn't match their biology.
Who weren't blessed with bodies that echo their heart
and soul.
And you get to cast shadows on their identity
by shining your incessant lights on mine?
Sir, you are most unkind
to try to define me
and my sisters.
To offer solace
on beds of knives.
To wear suits of armour
into vicarious battle
while real warriors
        wear only our skin
            and war paint.

Sir, your boys are sinking

in swamps of sorrow
of your own making;
while you train more knights
we train more witches.
You keep fattening up boys,
we bury them in ditches.
Those poor little lambs
so desperate not to become sheep;
sending them down rabbit holes,
filling their heads with
binary blacks and whites –
turning their souls gauzed-grey.
Fluidity of thought frozen
to solid unmoving structures;
ornaments on the mantle of minds,
picked up and held,
observed by consciousness
for reference,
but not scrutinised,
or moulded, by imagination –
    gathering dust as they
        get ignored
            into obscuration.

There is no further for us to fall –
we have fallen to our knees,
Into shallow graves.
Hell has been and gone through us
a thousand times,
and will a thousand more;

like passing armadas
collecting wenches
on the way to war.
There are no new ways to hurt us.
No fresh sufferance
worse than the countless
ones preached from your books:
the pious ones;
the fairy tale ones;
the ones where men cause havoc and destruction;
the ones where they pretend to make amends.

You can tell us how pretty we are;
as you are programmed to do so,
and we are indoctrinated to want.
Seek out our skin for sin.
Play the hunting games,
infer us as your prey,
but you cannot catch,
or contain us, anymore.
For, you gather strength
from the thought of things
you might do in future —
we take strength
from shattered pasts.
You wear pain for show —
crowns of fake thorns.
We wear it like diamonds
forged of hard scar tissue
from centuries of sufferance;

generations of damnation.

I don't want to come down
from hot high heeled majesty
to lukewarm temperatures –
to your tepid temptations.
You offer stoned memories
of mausoleum heartbeats;
A fossilised version of love.
While she
    –all of she–
    –all of we–
went to war for me,
before I even breathed mortal air,
before angels had wings,
before dragons didn't exist,
before love took a side,
before Mother
became Mother Earth;
    we were at war
    long before
    all of this.
We invented the language
of howling moons.
We have torn ourselves
through each December
just to slice ourselves,
again, in June.

Industrial Revolution

There is an entire industry
built around my pain.
Mace and pepper sprays,
hand held alarms,
daggers disguised as lipstick,
necklaces and rings
that serve as gps devices
which call family members
and the police
at the same time,
so they can race to the scene
and be the first to see me
dead or decimated.
Hide and go seek –
For the supposedly weak?
Locations turned on,
Just in case "something"
Happens.
Some.
Thing.
Some.
Body.
To find.   My body.
I grieve my virginity.
They will grieve what's left of me.
Every day we wake up and
have to C H O O S E
our own welfare,
along with our outfit of the day.
A silent agreement with our souls

because our tongues were stolen.
Those covers
I can put over my drink
so I don't get roofied
by a soulless perv.
As each petal is torn
I turn to my thorns
for prickly protection,
but thorns guard stems
not flowers on the ends;
and so remains
the top down destruction.
You can attend
Women only
Self-defence classes,
Because even the places
you learn to defend yourself
might feel triggering
if there are men around.
Learning to spell the word safe
with a fist and a kick,
because size does matter
in the game of dare:
dare I go for a run alone,
dare I put both headphones in,
dare I go out unprotected,
and be infected by the cycle,
of indoctrinated hate.
"Not all men, though!"
    I hear you say,

as if your absence
of aggression
cancels out rape.
As if not violating
another human
is an achievement
to be proud of.
What else do you celebrate
not doing?
Today, I did not rob a store
or commit fraud.
Tomorrow, I won't be
drinking and driving.
That's the difference
between men and boys:
men want credit
for the good things they do,
boys want a hug
for the bad things they didn't.

[Written collaboratively with Emily Willard]

Missing isn't the correct term;
I feel darker without her,
like there's a part of my being that
only switches on in her presence.

[extracted from my novel, Meticulous]

Sub Atomic

You are in my atoms;
last night I felt each cell
divide frantically,
scurrying,
exploding
in anticipation:
an automatic atomic reaction
    to our ethereal contract.

It's atomic,
and sub-atomic,
now –
our love.
Infinite layers
of decreasing sizes,
at increasing depths,
  going on
      and on,
          forever
              and ever;
an endless
Russian doll,
containing
our
love.

I make it sound
like a good thing
   (a good thing),
but it's bad –
Sickly bad –
to hold another in
your mortal engines.
To stall and stutter
without them flashing
through
every thought,
coursing through
capillaries.

Some might call it
poison,
venom,
a curse,
   addiction.

We call it love.

They speak of love
    with sugar coated
tongues -
    mouths full of honey
served on silver spoons -
as if love can't also flash
on the edges of knives,
    and slice
        through veins
            where glucose hides.

Real Eyes

Astrology didn't warn me about you.
Psychology didn't tell me what to do.
The raging red flags didn't shake me off your groove.
Oh, the atoms of my lonely heart they knew,
but the atoms don't matter when you're battered by
attraction.
Instincts are extinct when you're hook, line and sinker
caught on love.

I see you in the back of my eyelids.
At night, it curses me to non-sleep.
By day, I dare not blink in case I catch a peek.
When I want to see you I close my eyes,
close my mind
to the hurtful times.
Just a pretty perfect picture of a preened prince,
without the angry menacing grimace,
or my future scars held in his fists.

The lid-screens show only happy scenes:
whimsical whitewashed memories.
No splashes of bruised colour,
no hopeless hours of lost darkness.
Holistic, Hollywood, happy happenstances.

The eyes:
bluer than Olympus rivers,
soft as freshly emptied clouds.
I block out the redness,
ignore capillaries of soreness.

The hint of yellow intoxication
does not exist on love tinted lids.

The smile:
still subconsciously parts my thighs
as adductor muscles relax and sigh.
There's no tension in the recollection:
no feral forced penetration,
only a gentle lovers intention.
sweetly remembered seduction.

I recall only sensuous moans and groans:
you pleased in your pants every time you came home.
But you poured concrete down my throat,
guilt gargoyles snatch my tongue and I choke.
I can't speak truth of the other noises
caused by malicious marauding touches.

The arms:
romance novel masculine,
swaddling my feminine.
Holding the demons down,
NOT holding ME down.
Protecting me,
NOT hurting me.
NOT breaking me.

If I whisper: "I miss you," will you return?
The wounds still sting and burn,
but, behind the eyes, I'll never learn.

Ghost Host

How strange it is to dream of you
with eyes wide open.
The rhythm of my breaths
a dizzying disco in my chest;
lung beats and hate caked heart
bouncing pin-balled blood around
lonely love-lined veins.

The outright audacity of you:
to break and enter my mind,
time after agonising time.
I'm so bored of tears falling
on the memory of smiling
into your sharp shoulder blades,
hands roaming from neck to breast,
eager to little black undress –
forbidden, feminine, fornication.

You lied,
and you lie beside others so easily,
whilst my body quivers
under the shadow of us.
The creeping darkness
of your returning carcass
feels flinching distance
away.

Despite the history of hurt,
I'm still on the edge of burst
for your finger tip touches

on blushing hot skin,
aching for you to sin
inside me –
a taste of passion,
a splash of compassion,
a rainbow in the darkness.

I wish I'd written you –
that you were never real at all,
so I could un-write you from my narrative
with a finger tap on note pages.
I wish I'd said more
about the malicious ways
you cheated and betrayed,
instead of hanging on
for something extra that would never come.
I lived a regurgitated reality –
mouse-trapped in your myopic misinformation.

I am the definition of disaster,
a manifestation of mess;
dignity and self-respect
nullified by sadness.
It's a kind of tragic
framed by the grief of loss.
New clothes, same skin.
Lost virtues, found sins.

I envy the lucky leaves;
the ones that fold and die early,

not clinging to an unloving ghost host –
dwindling adoration never returned.

I have a message to my medicine:
the pills are not enough,
you are not enough prescription
to purge this gorgeous demon
from my mind and atoms.

It's more than a moment for me
    – It's all the moments –
lost and found wanting,
waiting.
Whenever never comes –
you never come.

Would I lie to you?
    Yes.
Would I burn for you?
    Yes.
Would I rather you died
than stayed hauntingly alive?
    Yes.

Rain

My window reminds me it's raining;
the glass beading fresh wetness.
Little globes of tears
sent from scar tissue of clouds.
I wonder if it hurts them
to release so much pain at once?
If they believe relief will follow release,
or they know death awaits?
Such sacrifice
the clouds give,
emptying themselves
to nourish the earth;
To nourish us.

I wonder if that's why
we try so hard
not to cry;
for fear that tears might end us,
or begin us, in ways
we can't contain.

My window reminds me it's raining,
and all I think about is you.
How pretty your cheeks blush
at the thought of summer storms –
the width of your smile
as droplets splash off wanton leaves,
and sink into thirsty soil.

[Dedicated to Stuti]

Love & Darkness

It's dark.
More than dark.
In every infinite direction.
Not dark like night-time;
dark like a place where day and night don't exist.
The bottom of deepest oceans,
where light gives up half-way.
There's only me
and the darkness
stretching forever.
A pin-prick of light
rages against the black canvas.
It's getting bigger;
I can't tell if I'm moving towards it
or if it's moving towards me,
but it's getting bigger.
The dot of light starts to take form;
from dot to collection of dots,
to blob of light,
to a vague notion of a body,
limbs and head,
the outline of a person.
It's you,

in all your beautiful ways,
wearing both our flaws
like war paint.
Like gold dust.
Like stardust.
It's always and forever you,
that infiltrates these dark spaces
reaching for me;
the real me
I'm supposed to be.
It's you who's belief
never falters.
When I push
you pull me back
from emptiness,
and fill the cup
with fresh heartbeats.
You are the pulse
that tethers me.
This time;
every time.

This is what love feels like.

[Adapted from my novella 'Girl on a swing']

Daring to Drown

It's taken these years
of starvation:
to understand
it was you
who fed my soul;

to understand
I wasn't a broken
sum of parts,
that I was always enough
and whole.

I've drifted so long
in blistering cold
to know
only your gentle scold
can thaw guilty bones.

Sometimes, forever
is just one moment,
to see myself
as you do:
not the wild outsider,
but the one you call your own.

I needed this much silence
to relearn your voice;
whether softly whispering
through kissing lips
or loudly howling
savage songs.

I learned
love is an anagram
for pain no more;
old scars found a salve
in your voice
when it whispered, I love you.

Love dies
as spring dies for summer,
it rises
as nourishing Solaris;
how many times
must it die and rise
until it falls on me?

I yearned for a blazing ball
of searing sunshine

but the moon —
cool and calm —
the moon was always enough.

I yearned for oceans
to rock me
in sweeping tides
But rivers —
rippling and rolling —
gently caressed
like your love.

Other lovers paddled
my shallow shadows;
only you dared
to drown in my depths.

Sinking in an ocean of emotion,
anchored to my every breath.

[Written collaboratively with Stuti Sinha]

Supposed to be a Love Poem

This was supposed to be a love poem,
full of heart-felt metaphors
comparing natures wonders
to the beauty of two souls
entwining with each other –
    speaking love language
    around campfires,
       eating marshmallows,
        drinking coffee with liquor,
       and falling,
   falling,
into heaven on earth.

Oh, there was the warmth of fire and flames,
    not the comforting kind –
the blistering heat of your abuse
still ghosts across my skin as scar tissue.
A map of malicious memories
tracing from neck to knees,
via sternum and vertebrae.
Your version of love language
    (spoken in Demonic tongue),
loud and slavering
angry and lost;
a boy without a fathers guidance
to steer direction or decency.
All testosterone and self-loathing,
    violence crackling on your skin.

This is the part where I'm

supposed to say
what happened made me stronger,
    but it didn't.
I learnt to move on,
    but I didn't.
You can't hurt me anymore,
    but you do.

Heaven will have to wait
until after this hellish life,
    between memories of the horror
    and compulsions to harm myself.

I had some freedom back then,
between the times
your limbs went wild.
In calm before storms,
in preface and aftermath,
    life was livable.

Freedom slips away over time
as hollowness turns to haunt,
as memories creep around every second.
That's why I sought others who hurt me;
to seek solace in the moments
between attacks,
rather than the relentless nightmares
    of never again.

Ghosted

I've been labelled a survivor.
I do not feel survived:
I feel stolen away
by the ghosts
floating still
on crystal waters;
toes tickled still
by the breezed
blades of grass
applauding us,
as we rolled our limbs together;
thoughts twisting still
like a hammock in a hurricane
unable to explain
why you left
from right.

I yearn for you
in the leaky love
of others –
search for you
In the cracks
of lesser lovers.
I ululate
madly
at the moon;
dry tears
at sunrise.

I mull, and I medicate,
    but only pain fades —
your image still
weaves its way
into the mist;
your voice still
    echoes,
    echoes.

You will not die
until I, myself, am buried —
the ripples of your tender
touch submerged,
consumed by worms.
The things we did
to each other
    exorcised
as whispers
on graveyard winds.
Even so,
I fear you'll haunt
my bones.

Never Heavy

There are days,
despite being afraid,
where I am feral;
savage and sacred.
Other days
I am
tucked up
in fetal position;
rocking in darkness,
hoping I find frequency
with the light.
There are times
a snake of shadows
helixes my body;
squeezing me tightly
until my lungs concede,
and I learn
not to breathe
wretched air.

I'd rather end
   (it all)
with precious memories
   (of love),
still fresh enough
to delude a heart
   (with hope),
than start again
without you.
The way I am

drove you away;
jaded and famished,
starved of attention,
deprived of affection.
You survived
my crushing clutches;
escaped
to a new lover
who knows how to pander
how to swoon,
how to stay clean minded
for you.

I tried to pour
the weight of woes
from my bones
so I could be
a lighter version of me.
A palatable husk;
a heatless, listless,
messy mass of flesh.
Mailable and compliant.
I tried to deconstruct
my muddled mind
so you could find
the me you deserved
me to be.
I tried to manage
my madness;
contain my calamities.

Be that thing
we both yearned
me to be.
I tried so hard
to be good,
    I forgot
    I wasn't evil.

I repeated so many
of your lies,
I forgot
how to be truthful.
You made me feel
so exotic and sexy,
I forgot the ways
you hurt me;
forgave the ways
you abused me.
The burgeoning burden
of possessive adoration
pressed down
    so   s l o w l y,
that it never felt   h e a v y,
until it snapped.

Mourning Prayer

I am dying,
as all creatures do –
but this is not death by ageing flesh,
not mere looming mort,
but mortification.
Slow recession
seeping into debt
to despair.
I die by inches every day;
by grams each minute,
by needles in my thoughts,
in the swirls of my mind,
aching to be visible,
yet invisible,
all at once.
Dreaming to be relevant
somewhere,
to someone,
yet unknown to small minds,
unseen by cancerous eyes.
Pleading for this cycle,
    (that I ride)
to release me.
To be held in your highest esteem –
lost in the chambers of your heart
forever;
yet, I never
let you know
until I couldn't.

Howling Aura

She had a howling aura;
like ancient agonies
of crimson moons
orbited her.

She had a flickering glow;
like wombed star-light
fought the darkness
around her.

She had a savage energy;
like blood tinted
winter sunrises
warmed her.

She had a feral face;
like wild beasts
locked horns and teeth
to woo her.

She had a pious anger;
like ordained commands
guided heathen hands
to crucify her.

She had a folded soul;
like tragedy and grief
had aggregated
within her.

She had a haunted smile;
like the ghosts
of future regrets
possessed her.

She had a lost spirit;
like forbidden stories
and muted songs
unwrote her.

We Were Warriors

We were warriors; not exactly wild and never really free. We staked claims to the small morsels at the sacrifice of bricks and mortal traditions.

.

We were warriors; fighting amongst ourselves for a place on slightly higher shelves, where the milk and honey is supposedly sweeter, and toil a forgotten noun not a living verb.

.

We were warriors; heroes of our own design and image. Saving the unsavable from themselves, selling false glory to ourselves, a sense of victory being enough to stem the thought that the gains were hollow and fought for naught.

.

We were warriors; full of youthful anger and virtue, devoid of any sin by way of lies and denial. We learnt to repackage our excrement as sweet smelling success – stories to feel and act superior. Souls sold and folded; owned and controlled pigs in shit.

.

We were warriors; lives on the line, freedom hung out to dry. We traded love for validation, causes for casual virtue. We marched our angry feet from the streets to our screens and played out fake wars behind them.

Wild Ones

In a different plane of existence,
far from this maddening world,
tripping through a timeline more suited to your quiet
grace:
the breeze would whisper wonder to the trees,
the trees would speak of magic things,
and everything—
life, death, and everything—
would be just a bit more bearable.
A little less heavy.
A little less messy.
A little less tragedy.
And the wild ones—
the ones you admire from afar—
who, like you, see beauty in moss
as much as stars,
would spin their words freely,
without fear,
without judgment,
without sanctimonious frailty.
It would all be a dance
In that place—
a dance instead of a chore;
and, at the end,
when terminal breaths blow,
even darkness feels warm.

Everything is grey.
	Not shades,
		just...grey.
One aching,
	soulless
	void.

Except you;
	you are in colour.

Monstrous Me

I sit silent waiting for November rain.
Outside, witches and spidermen chatter happily
through candied teeth.
I won't find relief;
    I imagine joining in.

The mirror mocks me as it always does:
I plan to dress-up as the worst monster I ever knew,
myself.
I can't wear the names they called me at school,
but they run through my mind while the makeup
paints past scar contours:
Slut…slag…hag…fat bitch…ugly bitch…stupid bitch.
    ALL the bitch combinations
    and humiliations.
I wish lipstick came in bitch;
    I'd so wear it.

My mind is in my teens;
I see, prettier girls than me
selecting costumes they afford so easily,
they wore so easily. Some tacky,
some sexy, none scary,
ALL for show –
Showing people like me
    we are not sexy,
    we are not worthy.

How was I so ugly to them,
yet so attractive to him?
I wanted them to be right:
pinned under his disgusting weight
like sacks of wet clothes pressing me down.
He'd tell me I was beautiful,
    while he made sure I wasn't.
He'd tell me they were jealous,
    whilst making a monster out of me.

He used to dress me afterwards
    (That was the worst part);
tracing fingers along quivering skin,
pausing to punish fresh bruises,
telling me I was beautiful
    when I cried.

I still cry
but no one tells me I'm beautiful.
Because I'm not;
    I'm a monster.
        His monster.

Adorned in mauve shadows
to blushed skin;
a kiss to the temple
sealing the deal.
His....
    I'm his.
        I'm his monster.

He would stand me in front
of my full length reflection,
twirl me like a ballet dancer –
    a Black Swan
        with a broken neck;
            no rhythm
                just prayers for death.

Curtain calls and dimming lights
can only mean one thing:
"Act Two."
I brace myself
    (cannot save myself).
Which should I hold this time:
    The face
        or
    the ribs?

I cried,
he smiled,
    and told me I was beautiful.

My smiles were real some days;
maybe I'm crazy.
He would say:
"We're Harley and Joker Baby,"
laughs born behind the eyes,
rejected from the heart.
    It's laugh or cry –
    cry or laugh.

Either way he wasn't satisfied:
hooked fingers inside my cheeks
forcing an Arthur grin.
"Daddy's little monster!"
He would say.
It was always
   trick,
      trick,
 trick.

Sweet unconsciousness was the only treat –
black out blinded was his favourite way.
Sometimes I'd mimic a corpse;
hold my breath,
(I'd practiced this daily)
in hope he would stop.
NO.
The ache pushed Into me:
HARD;
HARDER;
no push backs too,
because I'm supposed to
black out,
be silent while I was pinned
and passed around.
   This is what got him off

I still hear his whispers in the dark —
see his shape in shadows.
But I wear his darkness now
the way the ones with 'bitch' in their mouths
wear worn out frowns,
and dresses they can't afford.
Ghoulish games
the children played;
haunting their black hearts.

Halloween costume?
    Darling, I'm monstrous enough.

[Written in collaboration with Emily Langford]

Gentle Beasts

Some of them are gentle –
the beasts.
Gentle and kind,
but
  (with time)
they hold these traits
  against you,
like an IOU note.

Late at night
when sleep has
escaped you again…
A few drinks,
a soft compliment;
    "He must have been crazy…"
A few more drinks.
A few more words:
    "…to let you go."
Deeper conversation,
harder compliments;
the blushing kind.
Makes you feel special,
particular and precious.
Makes you a promise:
    "I'll never hurt you."

Compliment my bravery.
Tell me I'm fearless;
  I'm free,
whilst imagining I'm wild

(and savage)
    In bed.

Your silver feels golden.
Your heartbeat feels broken –
Like mine.
Like mine.
You're like me –
you like me.
No one likes me –
except you.

Make me feel wanted;
    (Wanton)
I'm not getting any younger:
    any thinner;
  any firmer;
any sexier.
Take the compliments
    while you still can.

Twenty years ago
his words would
have fallen
off his tongue,
landed in pools
of ravenous slime.
Now,
the same words
slither into ears

like a song
you pretend to love,
at a party
you're too old for.
   "I love this song, I love this song –
    Take my hand, we'll make it I sweaaaar
    Whoah-oooh living on a praaayeerrr."

It's his guilty *favourite* song too.
What a coincidence!
He matches your passions
with algorithmic accuracy;
mimics your pleasures
like a thought chameleon.
He finishes your sentences –
  your sentences,
    your sentence.
      your senses.
Mirrors your moods,
just like the songs
at parties,
he's got the right words
in the right order.
But –do you wonder
how many others, see the same words?
How many inboxes have pinged
the enticing tune?

How many hearts melt, under gentle heat?
How many finger tips, jump to his tenderness?
How many copy/paste mistresses
    cut open scar tissue –to offer their hearts?
It comes so easily; we're so easy
to deceive –ugly ducklings
waiting to be seen.
Tell us we're pretty,
make us your swan.
Tell us we're all the one.
Turn our necks
against our chests, (and each other)
until they break, on mutual hate.

Tell **me** I'm pretty,
promise not to trick me.
If I can't be THE one
at least let me BE one
    of many.
One is better than none at all.
Slowly, I fall, into you,
 fold myself, for you.

Promises skitter across
my follicles like spiders
casting webs, (of deceit)
thickening into grey cocoon,

until I can't move,
until I can't breathe
without you.

Endless waves of compliments
batter my jagged rocks
to pure white sand;
we walk (hand-in-hand)
through the paradise of my mind,
leaving footsteps where wetness
meets dry, where gentleness
meets tears.
You hear the fear in my music;
see the ache in my smile.
We walk for miles,
soles covered in sand,
crystal water lapping our toes.
Little schools of fish
expand and contract –
    black hearts in the ocean.
One of the others reaches out,
to **warn** me.
I get angry, I get sad,
I get mad (at her, not you).
She's a slut; a harlot. She's a liar.
She's jealous. She's not special,
like me.

We've got something special;
haven't we?
She's not like me;
I'm not a slut, I'm not a liar,
    You're not a player.
The thought of losing you
is worse than the horror
of sharing you.
You disappear for days –
that's okay, you need space
    to process
        how much you **love me**.

You and I are special;
we're different.
It's different;
we're special.

You bought me gifts.
  Held my hand in paradise.
    Saw the fear in my music.
      Held my hand in paradise.
        I owe you.
          I owe you.

You own me.

Stage Show

My whole life is a darkroom —
there are no walls to this hell.
No shadowed corners to hide in,
only curved lines looping
around blinding stage lights.
    (Shadows waltzing close behind)

By some measure I am noticed
and lights congregate on my frown.
    (Everything has beauty but not everyone sees it)
Performance becomes mandatory
In these scrolling screen dreams —
I am lead actor, director and producer,
yet have no control at all.
The source material is traumatic memories
and anxious, guilty thoughts.

Predatory flocks of circling birds
wait for carrion failures to feast on.
Pieces of flesh offered as prose and poetry;
lung beats sacrificed to a spoken altar.
Innards of intention lose mention
as white dove sentiments
succumb to raven claws.

I am ripped.   I am clicked.

 I am s c r o l l e d   apart.

I am seamless.   I seem less.

    I am screaming.

"Once Upon a Time"

"Read for me baby, read slowly."
"Even the scary parts?"
"Especially the scary parts."
"What if there aren't any?"
"We'll make some up."

I'm losing interest in everything again:
I see it all clearly,
I hear it all clearly,
but it's all so pointless
to me.
I don't **feel** any of it.
but it feels for me –
    predatory.

"Once upon a time a beautiful princess…"

The August sun spits itself through gaps in curtains on
to disgusting greasy skin.
Nightmare watch gives way to dreaded day dreaming.
Unenthusiastic breaths force feed my chest.
I'm not crying anymore;
the feelings haven't changed
but I'm bored of tears,
    bored of tears,
        nullified by sadness.

"She was the most beautiful in all…"

I quite like my features in half-light;

I enjoy the way my messy angles suit the looming
atmosphere.
In this silken dark,
the way I look suits
my hearts desires.

There's no rhythm to my thoughts;
they hit the wall of my dome
like a toddler banging the wrong toys together.
Some notions border on genius,
but I'm too listless
to make notes of the ideation.
    I'll curse myself later I'm sure.

"Evil witches had placed a curse on her…."

Conversation tastes like wine turning to water;
every ounce of fructose interest
fading to bland base elements.
There's a sharpness to my tongue,
a whip that waits to lash out at undeserving victims.
Cut their care and concern to hateful ribbons of:
        "leave me the fuck alone."

"…she was alone and afraid.."

The same songs ring in my skull as were rasped from
their lips before they punished me;
before they taught me consequence wasn't justice,
punishment didn't have to fit a crime.

Virginity wasn't a delicate set of petals
softly removed by cautious fingers.
It was a rotten forbidden fruit,
it's juices crushed by hands full of ugly power.
I didn't get to remember a nervous lover taste me for
the first time.
The lick language I learnt was of rough tongues
opening me up and spilling my innocence
over yellow canines.
Love bites were a literal description;
an actual clamping of teeth on delicate parts,
drawing blood which sometimes mixed with scared
piss.

"Who in all the lands could save her now?"

I wish I had a dollar for every stitch I failed to receive,
instead of a twisted scar tissue mausoleum.
No noble bones wish to lay to rest in this graveyard —
no flowers tribute my beauty.
Only this numbness festival which envelopes me at the
flick of a trigger.

"The Prince was the bravest and most handsome —"

"Why did you stop reading?"
    "I don't like this part; it's boring.
     Can we read the scary part again?"
"If that's what you want, baby. We can read them as
many times as you like."

Solitude

It's all about perspective:
to a child who enjoys
kindness in company
Solitude is full of dread,
    but
to a child for whom company means
violence and abuse,
solitude is a blessing.

When his amphibious hands peeled from my skin;
and his slimy (softening) member fell from inside me;
when he bid my mouth clean us from his phallus,
blood still leaking from broken nose;
when I couldn't breathe, but retreat was met with
brutal beats about my already bruised head.
When he made me say sorry
for almost choking to death –
    Was I lonely when it stopped?

Did I yearn for heroes,
constructed from television excerpts,
and brief momentary snippets of his goodness,
    to find
        and rescue   me?

When I peeled back my skin
to flesh and fat below
    exposing them to the edges
    of oblivion –
As the ideation of escape
flapped it's ecstatic wings,
did I dream of meeting others
    in the sky
        or flying on my own?

When yearning for a tender touch
from powerful arms;
aching to quiver under gentle weight.
Am I slut for wanting?
Is it wrong
(When it's been so long)
to imagine tongues
lapping orgasmic release –
afterwards
whispering sweetness
into my bones.
    Is that how it feels
    to be alone?

When I ask them to hurt me
in escalating ways:
to give me bruises
that feel so familiar;
open old scars,
inflict the agony I deserve;
call me the ghastly names
he invented;
punish me until I almost forget,
and roll
  their lack of love
    around me
Like a blanket of razor   blades.

When the walls I build
protect me from the good ones,
yet fold to ruins
when nefarious strangers call —
    Is it because I'm alone?

By Any Other Name

You painted me roses
but a rose is not always a rose.
Brushstrokes of untruths unfold –
wilted roses tinted noir;
soft petalled intentions
melting away to black tar.

Purple bruises
adorn skin canvas:
  A Cézanne of cruelty;
   A Matisse of beatings;
    A Monet of molestation.

You, the struggling artist –
creator of dark beauty,
murderer of souls
  (My soul),
carve your name into my bones;
a signature to own me with.

I, the aspiring writer,
wet between legs and ears.
Innocence plastered on tarpaulin,
spread out in sinister portraits,
framed on nefarious walls.

My skeletons were so heavy;
for, leaden are the bones of woe,
their pain with no place to go.
Molten marrow memories.
Sunken socket screams.

—Screaming in the driveway—

She carried death beautifully;
that candy caterpillar cutie
   (I used to dream I needed to be),
became a crucified chrysalis.
I've come to claim her ashes;
mould them into
bloodstained wings.
The pain is inevitable,
   In my past
      and your future.
She died in my nightmares,
   I   will live in yours.

Your rib infested chest
guarding the blackest heart,
hidden behind subversive art,

but
you are haunted by two things:
   -what you did to her
   -what I'll do to you.
Guilty flies feast flesh
until exposing bone.
Throat packed with roaches
choking on the horror:
   -of what you did
   -of others seeing
   -of being hunted down
   -of the monstrous butterfly you   made of me.

We'll never speak again:
you are my favorite stranger, now.

"A sprinkle of vengeance never hurt anyone"

YOU will become MY masterpiece now.

The world is better backwards.

Single Tear

They still think it was an accident;
a tragic distracted consequence,
caused by teenage clumsiness,
and too many intoxicants.

    I know better...

I sat there,
in those seconds of despair,
a bewildered spectator.

When I replay it,
slow motion in my mind,
It seems to take forever –
I wonder if
I could have leaped to the rescue?
Grabbed the gun;
  deflected her aim,
    at me
      instead of her.

Every daymare ends the same:
her dead
and me shaking.
I never save her;
most times I don't even try.
    I'm not sure why.

It's not blood, flesh or bone
I recall most;

It's the fallen features.
The suddenly vacant expression.
It's watching someone you know
slump out of existence
in front of your eyes,
    and behind theirs.

It feels perverse knowing I was the last thing they saw.
Sometimes,
(in the darkest moments)
I wonder
    if that was an honour
    or a curse.

You'd think fragments of skull
would be etched in my mind,
but it's the non-graphic details
that haunt:
    twitching of muscles,
    movement of the hair,
    specks of blood artistically splattered briefly turning
her face into an abstract masterpiece.
The smile;
the one you'd seen a thousand times,
but never with such finality,
Such peace,
and purpose.

A single tear escaped her eye

tracing down her cheek.
The only melancholic clue in an otherwise proud face.
The bullet shot the tear back through her eye socket,
through skull and brain,
and out the other side.

I prefer to poeticise It that way:
the bullet collecting her single tear
on its way through,
    growing wings and taking flight,
    releasing it to the heavens
        where it dissipates into cosmic ether.

On rainy days,
I wonder if her tears
are within the wet —
as a drop hits my face
I imagine there's a molecule
    of her
        within it.

I'll never know if that tear
fell from heavenly thoughts
or sought to soak hell.
All I know is:
    it never got to fall —
I hope it never will.

You can't always
be the lighthouse;
sometimes, you may be
the ship lost at sea.

Nightbirde

Out of sight;
a shadowed shape
against a sapphire sky.
 A night bird
 flaps it's wings
 and softly sings
 of hope,
 in tones unbroken
 by its pain,
to briefly show the world
what it means
 to be brave.
 To really feel alive;
 to spread sore wings
 proud   and   wide,

and fly,
 and fly.
 and fly.

Nightbirde – A truly talented woman who touched my soul with her courage and positivity despite her circumstances.

"Better Times"

It's our parents tepid gods
weighing heavy on our chests;
living up to decades gone,
lurching forwards to our deaths.

It's our ancestors bent backs
and stern judgmental eyes,
on brown & white photographs
from simpler, 'better' times.

It's 'the good old days'
spoken with liquored breath;
reminisce summer haze,
through rose-tinted specs.

It's the thought of having nothing
with dirty rolled up sleeves —
ideations of better things
ungratefully received.

It's tried and tired ideology
still swirling in our DNA.
Distrust of modern nuances;
mouths of salty retrograde.

It's stiff lips and gritted teeth –
or lifting fingers to a child.
Anger written in old cursive
remembered and glorified.

It's work 'ethics' of the past
indoctrinating the present.
Are blood, sweat and hard graft,
the only means to an end?

It's stubbornly held traditions
of fairy-tale institutions –
culturally ingrained decisions
and awkward conversations.

It's the ghosts of mistakes they made
haunting every inaction;
The shadows of the dues they paid
darkening good intention.

It's when men were 'real' men
and boys were 'just being boys';
It was all so 'polite' back then
when women were 'good' wives.

It's calling a spade a spade
to excuse the ethnic slurs.
Conditioned hate of 'the gays',
and talking down to girls.

It's valuing respect above love,
and fear ahead of kindness –
Taking guidance only from above,
instead of what's inside us.

It's their boom and bust addiction;
obsession with bulls and bears –
the trickle down delusion
which dictates today's affairs.

It's generational discourtesy;
remnants of harsher times –
fuses lit in children's ears
explode in adult minds.

Before You

Everything feels pointless
relegated next to you.
Each moment spent
absent of your eyes
grates tears to the ground.
My feet soak in puddles
of regretful seconds
    I'm not with you.

Earth becomes quicksand,
  And I sink
    down,
    down,
    down,
to the time before you —
    the empty void you filled.

My life is simply split in two:
    before I knew who I was,
    and after you arrived.

Latibule

The ghosts of unspoken words
hang so heavily:
ever haunting;
ever whispering;
ever wooing.
An unheavenly storm cycle
in this tortured
old mind.

The weight of could haves,
the mass of would haves,
the gravity of should haves,
burdened might have beens,
noose my existence.

But you…
you are my refuge;

my latibule.
Self-loathing's sweet salvation.
Regret and sin's redemption.

We sit…
your innocence;
your fluttering heart
pressed against mine.

Bitter memories of teenage angst
and fearful middle-aged laments
melt into forget
    and drift
        far away.

Snowflakes
on a summer breeze.

Baby Breaths

Lying here in fragile happiness,
hypnotised by cherubic innocence,
I inhale the newness of your scent
as I press my lips to your forehead.

Your sleeping breath
next to my nervous waking chest.
Your breathing free and light
as seraph sighs;
full of future promise,
empty of burden.
Just breaths –
  holding nothing more
or nothing less.

My own lungs bellow
deliberate and slow;
laboured, unsteady,
thick with creaking wisdom.
Tired and over-tested.

I look at you in awe
of the life which stands before,
and in ache
at the thought of pain finding you.

I do not want you to learn in harsh ways,
as I had to,

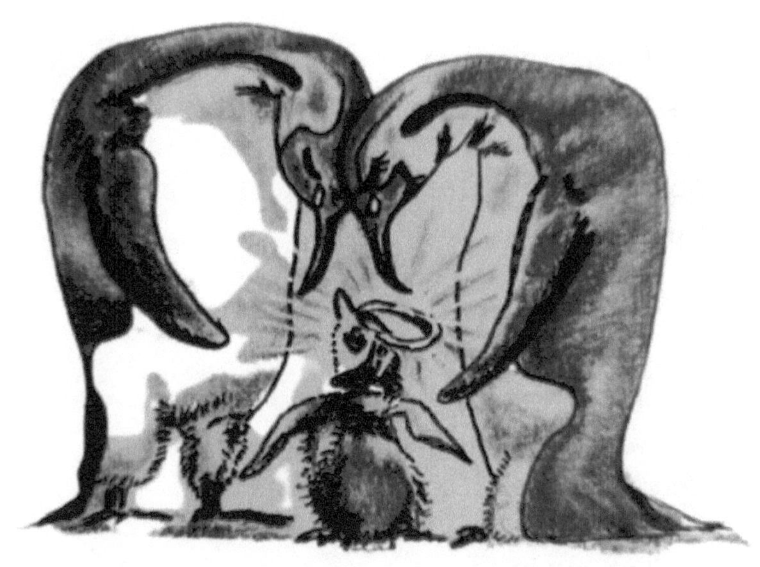

nor to only rise without any falls at all.
I desire to be your protector
with hope you need no protection.
My death holds no value
next to your trembling fate.

I want the life ahead of you
to hold the same contentment
as these hypnotic breaths;
    the dreamy ease of your breathing
        to last forever.

The weight of the moment folds around me;
I am suddenly shrouded,
in realisation that you
are the best thing in the whole world,
    with no close second.
My own breath quickens
to meet yours.
The beat of my heart flutters in fear;
I wonder between the beats
If either of us will be enough.
Who will carry who the most?
My energy catches fire on puerile flames –
I feel more alive than I've ever felt before.

[Dedicated to my boy]

Little Increments

Sometimes, the weight of shadows press heavy:
shadows of the lost ones –
angels you'll never know in mortal realm,
who I miss from the pit of my stomach,
in my skin and bones.
Their memory dances on my goosebumps
and leaks on to pillow cases.

The mess I become
in these moments
teeters on oblivion:
I am loathed of myself;
Infected by demons.
Dreams are sluggish and dark,
nightmares savage and cruel.
Life ebbs on around me
like a current passing a drowning bird.
Breath is sucked from my trembling lungs,
depleting my capacity to exist
in little increments with each exhalation.
Hope observes from long distance.
Happiness a fairytale held in other hearts.

The word 'self' divorces 'love' and 'care'
and seeks lusty dalliance with 'harm'.
Light falls away from me;
only darkest thoughts remain.

But you;
there's you.
For you it all subsides.
Already you have saved my life
simply by existing.

How unwise I feel looking into your bright blue eyes;
gargantuan caverns of unknowing resting upon my
shoulders.
Inept and impotent,
yet ready to try;
    to keep trying.

We both cry, head touching head:
    you, for the things you need to survive;
    me, for the things that didn't.

I feel like
I'm haunting myself.

Weightless

Today, I assembled household objects which added up to the same mass as you..

..and I held them tightly against my chest…

…just so I could reminisce
your weight in my arms.

I had no way to recreate your breaths,
but could still visualise them rising and falling your tiny sternum. I could hear the purring so clearly, and the rasps of your struggled breath.

Your little lashes and their unconscious quiver; making me wonder what dreams a teeny thing could be dreaming. I wonder if dreams exist where you are – wherever you are.

Your skin:
I swear I felt your skin against my fingertips and
forehead, as vivid as the days I actually did.

Your smell hit my nasal cavity just as if you were really
there,
sweetness intoxicating my soul.

The weight of you was enough to bring it all back.

As I tasted the tears fall to my mouth, it was a smile
they met.
  — that made me guilty: smiling doesn't seem the right
thing to do, but it is nether-the-less what I did.
    I smiled and remembered.

I wish your weight was with us,
or I could be weightless with you.

Flightless

Again,
your stolen wings
weigh heavy on my mind.

Why should your life have been so brief,
so flightless,
whilst I throw stones after stones
at this endless swamp of sorrow?

My pithy therapist urges me to find gratitude
(for the time we had),
which is vacant because it's worse
when I start to feel better.

Happiness,
is the monster under my fragile bed
where guilt lies waiting to strike,
where your disapproving shadow
casts subtle darkness over smiles –
healing holds hopeless hands for short hours,
letting go in the long dead of night.

Virtue seems sinful;
each kind act tainted by tragedy,
gestures empty and hollow,
conscientious pursuits misplaced against sadness –
  all shades of love

painted pale
  by your empty spaces.

I dare not take flight
when your wings never unfurled.
I dare not show hope
when you knew no such thing.
I dare not stop mourning
when all I have left
   is how your absence feels.

Numb;
my secret sweet spot;
neither glad of the life before me,
nor sad of the one taken.
Floating with storm clouds,
frightened of their thunder,
resigned to their rain.
Existing,
  (In a sense)
between what's lost and what remains.
Facing neither with courage,
wanting both to end.

Deathly grey hues hold safer views
than life's cruel colours.

Never Returned

I tried writing about you –
    the syllables became my grief;
about how you never flew
    but I only spelled out my misery.

I tried bleeding you on to pages;
    all that flowed was self-pity.
I tried portraying your precious face;
    all I described was agony.

I can't show you to the world
    because all they see is melancholy –
I showed someone your photograph,
    all they saw was tragedy.

I need to scream;
    tell them you are more than my sad story,
    worth more than my sorrow –
    more than their sympathy.

I want to explain
    how you were softer than anything I'd ever known

yet,
your memory is harder than stone —
how you brought me joy in
every short-lived breath
    but,
    they just said,
  "sorry for your loss."

That is how you are defined:
    framed by loss,
    known by grieving words,
    remembered in fallen tears,
    seen only as death and mourning.

    Not by your own beating heart
which fluttered against mine.
The wakening in your lapis eyes
that pierced me like no others.
    Nor by the flapping of your arms
when you first knew me as father
    from the others.

I didn't lose you;
    you were stolen –
the thief sits on a throne in paradise
excused by original sin.
    Or,
perhaps no shepherd oversees
 this bleak existence at all.
As insult to injury,
I plough this field of finality,
no harvest of answers
at the end to greet me.
Just this time,
  this space,
    this life,
to be eked out half-awake,
each second
seemingly stolen from you
never to be returned.
    Never to be returned.
        Never returned.

Knotted Bones

How can I think
    to grow,
    to keep going,
with knots
in my bones —
      with grief knitted
    to scar tissue?
How can I speak
of love and wonder
    whilst swamped,
    wallowing in loss —
  in your absence?
Can I dare
  to turn the corners
  of my mouth
  to a smile —
    for any while,
    express joy, or pleasure,
    without you to measure
     it with me?
How can I walk
          forwards —
       beyond this
     suffering stasis —
when movement
is held hostage
    by pain?
How can I dream
  of softer scenes
when stone

nightmares
     dust my chest —
how can I rest
in one sided beds;
  emptiness
     creeping into space
       beside me?
How can I trust
love's warmth
     to ever return,
     sitting frigid
     and feuding
       with my cold self;
     grounded
       to my old self —
how can I think
to grow?

[Dedicated to Angie]

Gravy Train

The sludge of existence
remixed and reinvented
on screaming black screens.
Blink, and you'll miss it;
the mortification of wishes,
the coaxing of wet dreams.
Words, placed in safe boxes,
tongues behind gritted cages.
Bent over versions of freedom;
gifted like a knife to a toddler.
Congruence of all thought,
originality sold and bought.
Wars, invented out of naught
end in coagulating dust.
The coldest souls complain
  about difference,
  about transition,
  about change.
The warm souls softly pine
  about loss, about love,
  about light, about (only) positive vibes.
The so called adults in the room
smile and swoon
through prescription gloom;

use belligerent brooms
to make sweeping changes
under carpets of censorship.
Sweep, sweep, sweep it all away;
the sparkly hues, the subtle shades —
poetic spectrums slowly fade
to lazy vanilla hazes.
Harmless, conformist musings:
black-on-white / white-on-black.
Click the next colourless extract.
Blur the piano keys to grey;
ebony and ivory became a train of gravy.
Add someone else's free music
   to boost that reach;
add fancy graphics
   for follower niche.
Welcome to the para-algorithmic,
self-esteem gymnastic,
meting flesh to plastic,
new world disorder.
Here is your uniform;
It's easy —
   just
      conform.

Samara's Pen

Samara grips a pretty pen
and commits fresh new crimes;
ones which forbid the feminine
from writing verse or rhymes.

The paper isn't illegal,
though made from slaughtered trees.
The pen isn't illegal;
a man can wield it free.

Guns in hellion hands,
they seem to break no laws,
and the theft of fathers land
bears no punishment at all.

Violating her unripe body
breaches no legislation,
but this pretty pen she holds
dooms her to annihilation.

Suddenly her existence
breaks draconian rules;
her, her pen and cursive
enrages fiendish ghouls.

The poppy fields down the road
are proffered military protection,
but her petal falls unguarded
under barbaric desecration.

Samara's mind now dangles
in hopeless, choking smog.
All her dreams embezzled
by malignant, marauding mobs.

Samara's pen is leaden now,
until last week it feathered –
she used to fly through paper dreams
which lie in ashen tatters.

Samara was the best in class
and showed such bright potential.
Now future mirrors mothers past:
an inkless, dreamless vessel.

"Education will set you free"
and for years it truly did,
but evil forced the teachers flee;
the rest were left beheaded.

The languages she learnt
can never pass her lips;
the books must be burnt,
even her journaled scripts.

"The pen is mightier than the sword"
So says the cliché phrase –
in the rawness of the real world,
ugly weapons rule the day.

The shadows of oppression
emaciate built-up trust.
Jagged rocks of regression
stone proud history to dust.

The beatings aren't illegal,
in forced matrimony.
The rape isn't illegal,
for she now belongs to he.

Samara smiles obediently
at her new disgusting husband.
She clings to prose and poetry
a risky, secret contraband.

Hope slowly bleeds away
as the ink drips to depletion,
but words can't be contained;
she keeps them in her conscience.

Thoughts without a canvas
drive young minds to abandon.
She numbs painful haze away
with opioid medication.

Samara's pen runs empty now
the ink reduced to null;
she places it inside a drawer
and reaches for a needle.

Safe Haven

There's a man who sits on a high horse
above all the fuss and mess,
he loves to offer solutions
to problems that don't exist.

There's a man who gawks at others
from a safe and far distance,
occasionally offering answers
to questions nobody asked him.

There's a man incased in a bubble
abroad from fear and risk,
sometimes casting judgments
on matters he knows no gist.

There's a man who sits on fences,
standing not one side or the other,
casting aspersions in both directions
then coyly ducking for cover.

There's a man who turns a blind eye
to the worlds dirtiest deeds;
as long as he is getting by
he turns the other cheek.

There's a man with no ideology
who mocks all those that care,
rejects that there's inequality;
from his view the system is fair.

There's a man with borrowed morality
but no compass to call his own;
he believes the concept of charity
should begin and end at home.

There's a man with smooth hands,
never callused by toiled earth.
He speaks in tongues of grand plans
while others do all the work.

There's a man with shiny shoes,
and soft unscarred fists.
He tunes in to media news
and regurgitates the bullshit.

There's a man scrolling screen feeds
who claims he knows it all,
quoting media inventions
without an original thought.

There's a man who preaches to a choir
never challenged, or filtered his words;
spitting out platitudes of faux desire,
worshipped by unthinking herds.

There's a man with fake conviction
who blathers out hot air –
never taken any action,
leaving arse shaped dents in chairs.

Feels Dealers

We peddle pain and sorrow
for love and adoration.
We sell these poetic souls
for clicks and affirmation.

I'll trade you these lines
for a hit of validation;
clever flows and rhymes
begging for recognition.

I'll tear the woe right from my bones,
extract each drip of emotion;
present it all in heartfelt prose,
preached to the congregation.

Harness that love and hate
in to smart rhythmic beats —
noose my mental health
so my ego feels replete.

It's primal and raw;
torn from my atoms.
Never seen before;
give you brain-gasms.

My mind is all yours –
come take a look.
Just give me endorsement
of my war-torn book.

My thoughts you can traverse
from virtue through to sin;
I'll do flowery or perverse
as long as I'm "winning."
If I wrote it while crying
would you give it a like?
If I write it while bleeding
would you click on my link?

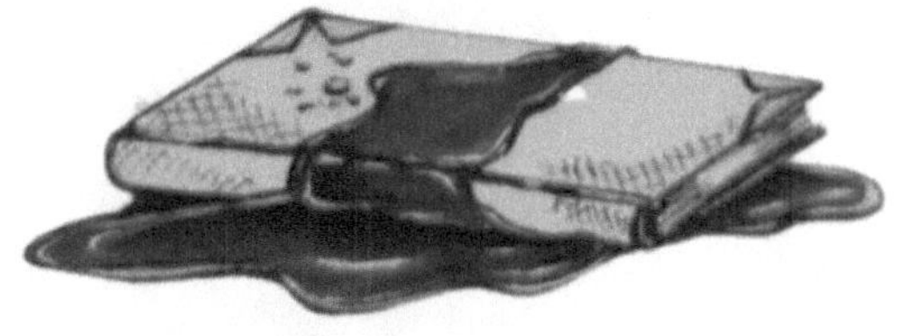

Golem

I don't feel birthed;
I feel wombed from earth's crust—
Sculpted from ancient dust—
passed down endless eons
through generations
of joy, despair,
loss and hope.

A golem, I am,
of clay and mud,
moulded by heathen hands,
in some unseen mighty vision.
Petrified and ugly;
An empty vessel
with nothing to contain
but swirling sands
of black emotion,
devoid of neon thoughts,
doomed to dally in darkness.

Somewhere in that infinite inner,
strings of words
float like gossamer—

a galaxy of gossamer
Inside of me.
Thick fingers of thought
trawl the vortex—
Spinning, spinning;
weaving silicon with silk
until primitive images
form at centre of mass,
like candy floss thickening on a stick.

Some thoughts fetter
as muddied, maddening words,
chasing sedimentary cheers
and the claps of pious hands.
Out of mouth,
or scrawled in ink,
on scrolling walls,
words either stick
or fall away.
And what is left
clinging like limpets
to existence—
We name poetry.

Heavy

Heavy
Silence is heavy.
   Noise is heavy.
It's all heavy:
   existing,
      breathing,
         knowing things,
            not knowing things —
lead weights
   pulling me down,
            down,
         down,
      foot to floor,
   chin to chest,
eyes to the ground
         down.

[Dedicated to Kristin]

Not Poetry

You impolitely told me
what I write isn't poetry;
words like mine
are destroying the art.

How flattered I was
that you thought me
important enough –
potent enough –
to collapse an entire
Kingdom of expression
with just my words.

Such esteem
you must hold me in,
to consider my free verses
so powerfully subversive
that they may rise up,
from the ashes of poetry,
and rule a new creative dynasty.

Maybe I'm a word Messiah
of poetry and prose;
sent by the gods
to festival the new
and consecrate the old?

At least, I think that's what you meant?

Then I looked at your page
and chuckle-choked
on my Caffè Americano.
There you were in all your inglory
wearing red flags like jewelry,
writing poetry as if it were
a bed sheet to be folded
neatly and placed in a drawer
with all the other beige cotton.
I wonder if you've ever
caressed silk or satin –
lay out under night skies
with no order except the stars?
I wonder, have you listened
to whispering breezes,
or waves crafting rocks
In to sand?
I wonder, if you feel love
skip over follicles,
or bounce around
In a racing heart?

I wonder, if you'd tell
a mother
she failed to raise a child,
as easily as you chastised me
for birthing my words?

I wonder, if you've
ever tied a ribbon
to something
and made a wish
for someone else's happiness?
I wonder if you've known
happiness at all;
or, like poetry,
it sits so far from
your soul
that you lash
and spit at others,
plotting their demise
to match your own?

A.I.

I was asked today
if I'd checked out art
created by artificial intelligence.
Are there not enough
starving artists already?
Are we to trade
a convenience of speed
for a loss of feeling?
The end product
on my screen;
is it to be priceless
or just worthless?

Am I to imagine
that sorting lines of code
onto shelves of emotion
equates the same
as pulling pain from
depths greater than
ones and zeros?
A gift can't be uncoded,
or downloaded,
into extracts of
expression.
Without a heart
it's not art.
Without a soul
it's fools gold.
Without love
it's just an image,

to twitch a finger at
while scrolling,
   scrolling,
   scrolling.

The best artists
may be dead
but at least they
were alive
at one time.
At least they felt
the darkness
chasing after them,
willing them
to create,
and create,
before life fell away
from the brief window
infinity afforded them.
At least they understood
the need to weave
the universe
into stories,
before there were no more
stories to be told.
At least it mattered
to someone.

Funny little life

Some days
my heart is almost static;
begrudgingly slugging blood from chest
to the rest
of my hopeless, molested mess
of a carcass.
Other days,
it races like a runway train,
spinning me to a giddy daze –
I'm dancing wild-footed and free.
All the static builds to a charge of electric ecstasy;
pumping pulmonary passion passenger trains through
zealous veins.
It feels as though seeds are growing
in my stomach,
and flowers might burst from my scars;
bees upon the breeze
will collect my agonies on their knees,
turn tragedy to honey

in their funny little hives.
What funny little lives
they lead.
The petals fall away
day-by-day,
slowly folding hope
to decayed remains
of better yesterdays.
Stasis finds me hopeless again.
As for the runaway train:
it becomes the bipolar express —
next stop un-hot mess.
Resentful depression
undresses the reverie.
The flowers stop blooming.
The bees only sting.
But I'm dancing,
dancing.

Imago

Do you suppose a butterfly,
in majesty and splendour,
considers lowly dust mites
as it glides from flower to flower?

Do you suppose a butterfly,
polychromatic and vivid,
spares colourful passing thoughts
for the larva sitting livid?

Do you suppose a butterfly,
gorging on fruit and nectar,
remembers the waste and lichen
it devoured as a caterpillar?

Do you suppose a butterfly,
floating free on spring breezes,
considers the chrysalis prison
that guarded winter freezes?

Do you suppose a butterfly
caught in hellish nets,
curses the gods artistry
that gave it decadence?

Do you suppose a butterfly,
paraded in a glass jar,
laments metamorphosis
that gifted doomed allure?

Do you suppose a butterfly
pinched between thumb and finger,
dwells upon the coming fate
and on its sadness lingers?

Do you suppose a butterfly
needled to a white board,
invokes the weeps of angels
mourning beauty torn abroad?

Speak my name
only when you have
earned the right.
Let not it fall
from idle lips
without intent
to massacre me
with passion.
Keep my noun
deep down,
below your throat
unless,
in its telling,
   you wish
   to set me free.

[Dedicated to S.A.Quinox]

Decibels

They measure screams in decibels.
I present them in syllables.
The louder the agony,
   the harsher the words.
The fresher the blood,
   the sharper the verse.

I've been asked why I didn't struggle;
why I didn't fight back –
I did.
I did.
I did.
Until I didn't.
I'd given in.
     everyone gives in…
eventually.

Do you know how acquainted with hurt you can
become?
  – I do –
You can be so accustomed
that you treat it like meditation:
lay back, relax, do some breath work,
plan your appointments.
I'd have filed my nails if my hands were free

and if he hadn't made me cut them short;
long nails are for sluts, everyone knows that.
And hair.

I started to write poems
while he was digging into me.
They were really romantic and sweet,
about fresh young love –
puerile and free.
I imagined we were real lovers;
consensual and caring.
He actually craved me,
rather than violated me.
The first thrust was met
with my wetness and want,
rather than dry excruciation.
He placed his mouth on me
to tell me my pleasure mattered –
that I mattered.
Asked me, so sweetly,
if it's okay to touch me
        here;
to kiss me
            there.
If I'd like to try something new.

If I was enjoying it.
If I was okay.

   Are you okay?
   Are you okay?
   Are you okay?

Soft new lovers suffer for his sins:
turned away from my body;
turned away from my alter;
I won't allow them to worship me –
   I
     am
        not
           worthy.

I kept the poems in my head
until he snorted in his sleep,
and down stairs I'd creep
  to write it all down;
  to write him all down.
Combining pen and paper
wasn't always cathartic enough –
some feelings were written into skin instead,
with a knife that deserved to plunge into his chest.

"You're lucky," they said, "At least you made it out
alive."
As if alive is an achievement.
As if escaping death belongs on a résumé.
As if my breath and beating heart are fair exchange for
being mutilated.

Do you know it is possible to be dead and alive at the
same time?

Dead inside the mind but the mechanisms of breath
and blood keep whirling around and around.
Often, I'd rather be dead, than sit listless waiting for a
window of hot calm to live within.

They measure screams in decibels,
but screams sighed in airless silence,
    (that never quite make it past the teeth)
are the loudest ones,
are the saddest ones.
    Hiding under sleepless blankets;
    recoiling from happiness.

Mirror

I look at the ghost in the mirror –
she stares right back at me.
We both have the same olive skin
and our almond eyes
bleed the same hue.
Pulling out the same pretty daggers,
she licks our white noise off of the glass.
We taste like the last time we met;
when we fought and fucked and love-hated our
trauma into each other's life sentences.
Till death due us part,
one tombstone, two heads at rest.
It smelt of burnt flesh and our sins and regrets buried
in the pits of our regurgitating stomachs.
We can't breath – its water where she is;
where we lay in our waste.
Our lungs are filling with wet memories that our brain
has yet to delete from our hard drives.
She drives her rage inside of me.

She fxcks me like she loves me but instead she's so
insecure she has to hack my system to find out who I
speak to in private;
 breaking my trust completely —
suffocating from atom to bone.
I don't want to save her anymore
but I must.
I love her the way the ocean loves clouds;
the way trees love soil.
I love her in and out of her skin,
the way a man should love one woman
    if only he had learned to love himself first.

[Written in collaboration with M.Hutman]

Mama Bird

A little birdy
once told me
it was morning;
it would twitter
at the rising sun
announcing itself
to potential mates.
Every goddam day.
I used to resent
the existence
of that bird;
blue and cute
and up for the worms,
daring to disturb
my precious sleep.
My fragile peace.
My sacred silence.

I miss laughter;
there is no laughter here.
It exists visually
as wide-open mouths,
nodding heads,
and rasping lips
that look like fish
feeding through a river.

The memory of music haunts me;
only a watered down
version remains,

like my brain is a tin can
full of the ocean.
When I try to recall
a specific song,
or just a note,
memory stretches,
and thins,
as though the music sits
on a piece of gum
being pulled out
from my mouth;
away from me
in ever increasing vagueness.
No, there is no music here
only wet echoes of wailing ghosts.

I wish there wasn't the version of me
that sang and played piano —
that she wasn't so fucking good at it;
or at least, had been confirmed a failure.
That would help;
knowing my dreams weren't real.
But they were real.
They weren't even dreams;
they were a destination
I was heading towards.
I would drum out success
with rhythmic fingers.
until the drums
in my head

stopped beating.

I would take that moment right now
despite the agony and fright.
I would happily relive
that torrid moment like Groundhog Day
as long as I could hear it.
I would trade a thousand
screams of agony
for this noiselessness.

My life is a Venn diagram
of fishbowls.
I can function on your screen
as long as you don't need
to hear my voice,
or I yours.
I can be a lifeless soul
of any party.
I can read lips
until the lips forget
I'm reading them.
Conversations are like trying to track
racing cars around a dusty course;
one slip of concentration
and the whole thing falls from view.
I become a ghost in the room:
a sliding shadow
doing its best to
clutch on to clues.

I become a burden
to kind hearted friends,
who try so hard
to constantly remember
to include my condition.
But my inclusion
ends up haunting the situation.

Silence is golden,
so goes the expression.
When you are deaf
you don't get to feel silence.
Silence is that serene sensation
when the din of the world
dissipates away,
and you can just lay
Tranquil and…
that feeling doesn't exist
for me.
Just as a blind woman
cannot know the relief
of closing her eyes.
There is no silence
to escape to –
only silence to suffer within.

What about some simple things?
There is no sound of coffee brewing,
no scratch of pen on paper,
no creaks of old floorboards.

no sound of letters sliding into post boxes.
or no sound of a man sliding inside me.
You know that sound when you suck a cut in your
finger,
somewhere between a kiss and slurp?
Or, to be more crude,
when you suck something else –
I miss that;
the sensual sounds of love making
or the frantic slapping noise of fucking.
I don't hear his excitement,
or my own climax.
There are shadows where moans should be,
and ghosts on the lips of "I love you."

Afterwards;
the sound of his piss
pelting the toilet
once a nuisance
now, would be a comfort.

What do I miss the very most?
The sound of my children.
Doesn't matter doing what;
just the audio accompaniment
of their very being.
I miss knowing they are hurting
from slight crackles in their voices,
or knowing their anger
from huffs and puffs

and the slamming of doors,
or knowing the intended tone
of the word "mama"
    Mama I'm back…
    Mama can I have…
    Mama come see…
    Mama I'm sorry…
    Mama I fucked up…
    Mama I'm scared…
    Mama I'm here…
    Mama I love you…

The bird had a mama too,
who'd listen to it warble
demands of warmth and food.
I wonder if she ever got sick of listening?
I wonder if she ever wished for its silence?

I lie in soundless ache
just wanting to wake
with the birds.

[dedication to my friend Mira Hadlow]

I Do Not Love You

I do not love you
in safe ways,
with clean hands.
I do not love you
in calmness—
seas rolling
freshly spun satin
over trippy toes.
I do not love you
if love is only
photogenic moments—
doubtless, faultless—
not careening down
mountain roads,
wind thrashing faces
frightened, to be alive.

I do not love you
in happy ways;
I love you aching
and mortified—
stripped bare
clueless and scared.
I love you when
love might tear
us apart,
cast our flesh
to hungry gulls.
I love you in the ocean
on its wildest days;

in weather warnings
blizzards, hurricanes.

I do not love you
In warm ways,
kissed by Spring.
I do not love you
If love may
not feel frozen;
shatter to pieces
under the weight
of a careless touch—
frigid and afraid,
that it might
melt away
to Summer's heat.

I do not love you
In wedded ways—
In finger rings,
and written vows.
I do not love you
if love is a contract
between promise
and hope.
I do not love you
In hopeful ways;
no, I love you hopeless,
folded by the world,
stretching yourself

thin, between duty
and grace.
I do not love you
in tidy order;
everything placed
as wished by dreams—
I love you drowning
In fear and mess;
I love you lost.

I do not love you
in living ways;
breath blooming
in eager chest.
I love you close to death—
in breathless memorandum,
in wilting weakness.
I do not love you
if love cannot mourn
the ones we lost,
who knew our name
as a single thing;
a single fragile thing.

I do not love you
In loud pressing ways,
howling adulation
as wolves to
the moon;
bleating adoration

in soulless serenades—
I love you out of sight
with quiet mind,
in silent reverence.

I did not love you
at first sight,
I loved you thereafter—
incrementally by day
exponentially by embrace.
I loved you on arrival,
I'll love you as you leave.
whether finding better
rhythm for your heart,
or upon its last beat.
Should you die, before I,
I'll love you in death;
in soil and dust—
your grave, your ghost—
haunt me, I beg you.

I do not love you
in safe ways.

[Dedicated to my wife]

When I Met Poetry

I met her in a raging storm
on a rainless summers day.
I met her where dreams are born
and nightmares break away.

I met her in predatory light
glinting on sands of time.
I met her in the losing fight,
and reached to make her mine.

I met her breath in my chest,
her oxygen in my heart beats.
I felt my life begin afresh
when I met my poetry.

Don't waste your magic
on non-believers.

About the Author

D.L. White – AKA Danny Boy – Is an Anglo-Irish novelist, writer, and poet. A loving husband and father with a passion for words in all forms. He has published several works, from poetry collections to full-length novels.

Outside of writing, he finds joy with friends, family, books, and thoughts of travel. He is a committed advocate and ambassador for mental health, working on a volunteer basis to support people with their battles, having battled his own demons his whole life.

Connect with D.L. White
Twitter: DL_White_Author
Instagram: dlwhite_author
Facebook: D.L. White
TikTok: dannyboywrites